CESC
SPRT

W9-BHZ-948

BASKETBALL
RECORD BREAKERS

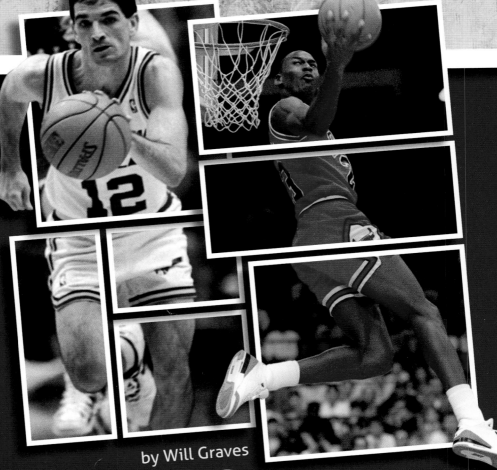

by Will Graves

SportsZone

An Imprint of Abdo Publishing | abdopublishing.com

abdopublishing.com

Published by Abdo Publishing, a division of ABDO, PO Box 398166, Minneapolis, Minnesota 55439. Copyright © 2016 by Abdo Consulting Group, Inc. International copyrights reserved in all countries. No part of this book may be reproduced in any form without written permission from the publisher. SportsZone™ is a trademark and logo of Abdo Publishing.

Printed in the United States of America, North Mankato, Minnesota.
042015
092015

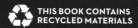

Cover Photo: John Swart/AP Images, cover (right); Steve C. Wilson/AP Images, cover (left)
Interior Photos: John Swart/AP Images, 1 (right), 23; Steve C. Wilson/AP Images, 1 (left), 20; AP Images, 5, 13, 14; Paul Vathis/AP Images, 7, 8; WGI/AP Images, 11; Douglas C. Pizac/AP Images, 17; Mark J. Terrill/AP Images, 19, 27; Matt Sayles/AP Images, 24; LM Otero/AP Images, 28; Kathy Willens/AP Images, 30; Kirthmon Dozier/AP Images, 33; Fred Jewell/AP Images, 35; Mark A. Duncan/AP Images, 36; Winslow Townson/AP Images, 39; Elise Amendola/AP Images, 40; Charles Krupa/AP Images, 42; David J. Phillip/AP Images, 44; Bill Janscha/AP Images, 45

Editor: Patrick Donnelly
Series Designer: Nikki Farinella

Library of Congress Control Number: 2015931671

Cataloging-in-Publication Data
Graves, Will.
  Basketball record breakers / Will Graves.
    p. cm. -- (Record breakers)
Includes bibliographical references and index.
ISBN 978-1-62403-846-4
1. Basketball--Juvenile literature. 2. Basketball--Records--Juvenile literature.
I. Title.
796.323--dc23
                                                                  2015931671

TABLE OF CONTENTS

Note: All records in this book are current through the 2013–14 NBA season.

100 WONDERS

Wilt Chamberlain was one of the first true superstars of the National Basketball Association (NBA). Standing 7 feet 1 inch tall, "Wilt the Stilt" towered over most opponents.

But Chamberlain was more than just a big guy. He was an athlete. During his college career at the University of Kansas, he was a member of the track and basketball teams. Chamberlain even won the high jump in the Big Eight Conference track meet three times.

Wilt Chamberlain used his height advantage and athletic skill to dominate his opponents.

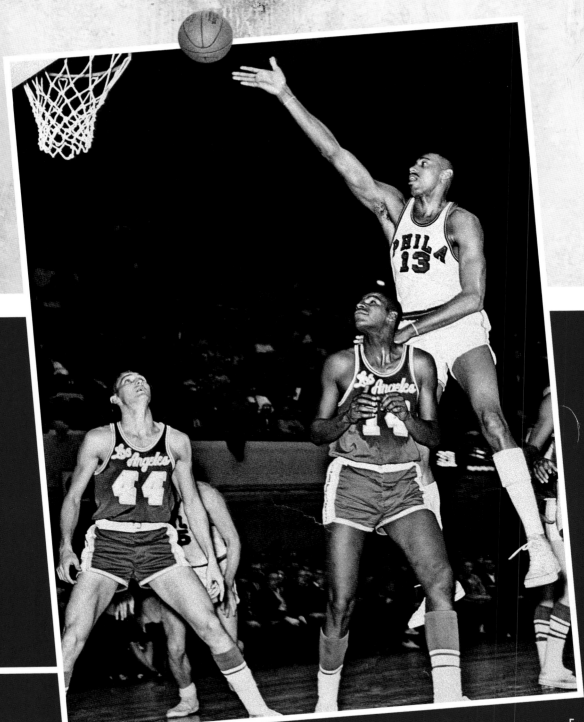

Chamberlain saved his best jumping for the basketball court. He made an instant impact when he joined the Philadelphia Warriors of the NBA for the 1959–60 season. He won the NBA Rookie of the Year Award after averaging 37.6 points per game, the most ever by a first-year player.

But Chamberlain was just getting started. By his fifth year he was the best player in the NBA. One night in 1962, he made history.

Even though Chamberlain was famous, the Warriors had trouble getting fans to come to their games. A few times a year they would play home games in Hershey, Pennsylvania, a smaller city two hours west of Philadelphia.

Most games were not televised back then. And only 4,124 people made it into the Hershey Sports Arena on that rainy Friday night of March 2, 1962. Those fans were the only witnesses to Chamberlain's historic performance.

The Warriors were facing the rival New York Knicks. The Knicks were missing center Phil Jordon, who was out with the flu. That meant backups Darrall Imhoff and Cleveland Buckner were left to guard Chamberlain. The matchup was a mismatch.

Chamberlain scored 23 points in the first quarter. The total jumped to 41 by halftime. The Knicks tried to guard Chamberlain with two players. He kept right on shooting. He poured in 28 points in the third quarter. That gave him 79 for the game. That was already more than the record 78 points he scored in a three-overtime game against the

Fans and teammates pour onto the court to congratulate Wilt Chamberlain after the Philadelphia Warriors center scored his 100th point of the night on March 2, 1962.

Los Angeles Lakers earlier in the season. Philadelphia lost to the Lakers that night. Chamberlain made sure it did not happen again.

The crowd chanted, "Give it to Wilt," and the Warriors kept passing to their star. The Knicks tried everything to stop Chamberlain. They even fouled other Philadelphia players to keep the ball out of Chamberlain's hands.

Nothing worked. Chamberlain was in the zone. He did most of his damage close to the hoop, naturally. But he even hit a few long jump shots and fadeaways. His thirty-sixth

Wilt Chamberlain holds a sign denoting his 100-point game on March 2, 1962.

field goal came with 46 seconds left and gave him
100 points. No player has ever scored more in a game.
Chamberlain made 36 of 63 field goals. No player had ever

taken or made more shots in a game. He was normally a poor free-throw shooter, but that night he made 28 of 32 at the line.

Philadelphia won the game 169–147, but there is no video of Chamberlain's magical night. The most famous evidence of his efforts is a black-and-white photo of Chamberlain holding a piece of paper in the locker room with the number *100* written on it.

The smile on Chamberlain's face makes it seem like even he could not believe what had happened. His teammates and the rest of the NBA felt the same way.

KOBE TAKES OVER

THE LOS ANGELES LAKERS WERE TRAILING THE TORONTO RAPTORS BY 18 POINTS IN THE THIRD QUARTER ON JANUARY 22, 2006. KOBE BRYANT WAS MAD. THE STAR GUARD DECIDED IT WAS TIME TO TAKE OVER.

BRYANT SCORED 55 POINTS IN THE SECOND HALF. HE HIT THREE-POINTERS. HE DUNKED. HE MADE FREE THROWS. ALL THE RAPTORS COULD DO WAS WATCH. BY THE TIME BRYANT WALKED OFF THE FLOOR, HE HAD 81 POINTS, THE SECOND-HIGHEST SCORING GAME BY A PLAYER IN LEAGUE HISTORY. JUST AS IMPORTANT TO BRYANT, THE LAKERS HAD A 122–104 VICTORY.

2
TWO PERFECT MONTHS

The Los Angeles Lakers were the best team in the Western Conference in the 1960s. But they could not seem to get over the hump.

The Lakers lost in the NBA Finals seven times in 10 years. By 1971 they had grown tired of coming up short. Los Angeles hired a new coach named Bill Sharman. Sharman was a former All-Star who had won four championships with the Boston Celtics. He knew his job was to take the Lakers to a title. Sharman looked at a roster filled with talented players such as guard Jerry West and center Wilt Chamberlain. He thought it was time for the Lakers to change the way they played.

Lakers guard Gail Goodrich drives past two Philadelphia 76ers as teammate Wilt Chamberlain looks on in the background.

Sharman told his players that if they passed the ball and played fast, no team in the league could keep up with them. Not the Celtics. Not the New York Knicks. Not the Golden State Warriors. Sharman promised his players that if they listened, the Lakers would be winners.

Los Angeles got off to a quick start, winning six of its first nine games. Everything clicked on November 5, 1971. In their tenth game of the season, the Lakers beat the Baltimore Bullets 110–106. Six players scored at least 10 points that night. It looked as though Sharman was right. When the Lakers shared the ball, they were tough to stop. It was a sign of things to come.

The wins started to pile up. The Lakers ran, passed, and shot with ease. Chamberlain gobbled up rebounds and fired long passes to open teammates streaking down the court. West and fellow guard Gail Goodrich usually turned those long tosses into easy layups before the other team could get back on defense.

The faster Los Angeles played, the faster the victories piled up. The Lakers won all 14 games they played in November. They scored at least 103 points in each. Then they kept winning. On December 10 the Lakers played in Phoenix with a chance to win their twentieth straight game. That would tie the NBA record. Los Angeles took a 12-point lead into the fourth quarter. The Suns rallied to send the game to overtime. With the streak on the line, the

Wilt Chamberlain prepares to throw a long outlet pass to a teammate to start another Lakers fast break in a 1972 game against the Portland Trail Blazers.

Lakers outscored Phoenix 15–6 in the extra period to match the mark.

Two days later the Lakers set a new record with their twenty-first consecutive victory. And they kept on winning. They scored 154 points in a win over the Philadelphia 76ers to push the streak to 25. A few games after that, they crushed the Seattle SuperSonics 122–106 to make it

Lakers point guard Jerry West drives past a Houston Rockets defender as Wilt Chamberlain, *left*, sets a screen in a 1971 game.

30 straight. Most of the games were not even close, with the Lakers winning by at least 10 points.

The Milwaukee Bucks finally snapped the Lakers' streak at 33 straight with a 120–104 win on January 9, 1972. It was the first Los Angeles loss since Halloween.

The defeat was merely a speed bump for the Lakers. They went on to win a total of 69 games in the regular season. That was a record that stood until Michael Jordan and the Chicago Bulls broke it in 1995–96. The 1972 playoffs ended up looking a lot like the regular season. Los Angeles raced to the NBA title, beating the Knicks in five games in the NBA Finals. It was the Lakers' first championship since 1954, before they had moved from Minneapolis to Los Angeles. The season stamped the 1971–72 Lakers as one of the best teams ever.

RISING HEAT

FEW TEAMS HAVE CHALLENGED THE LAKERS' EPIC STREAK OVER THE YEARS. LEBRON JAMES AND HIS BUDDIES DWYANE WADE AND CHRIS BOSH CAME PRETTY CLOSE WITH THE MIAMI HEAT IN 2013. THE HEAT RIPPED OFF 27 WINS IN A ROW IN FEBRUARY AND MARCH OF THAT SEASON. THE RUN ENDED WITH A 101–97 LOSS TO THE CHICAGO BULLS. BUT THAT WAS JUST A MINOR SETBACK FOR THE HEAT. MIAMI WENT ON TO WIN A TOTAL OF 66 GAMES DURING THE REGULAR SEASON AND ENDED THE YEAR WITH A SECOND STRAIGHT NBA TITLE.

3
A PASSING
FANCY

During his 13 seasons in the NBA, Earvin "Magic" Johnson turned passing into an art form. While Johnson was basketball's Picasso, John Stockton was more like a house painter—an efficient, effective, and wildly successful house painter.

Johnson always made things interesting on the court. Behind-the-back passes. No-look passes. Between-the-leg passes. If there was a fancy way for Johnson to get the ball to a teammate, he was going to find it.

Johnson also played with some of the greatest players ever while running the point for the Los Angeles Lakers in the 1980s. Playing alongside the likes of center Kareem Abdul-Jabbar, forward James Worthy, and guard Byron Scott, Johnson usually found someone streaking to the hoop. Those easy baskets helped make Johnson the NBA's all-time assist king.

But his reign did not last long. John Stockton could not have been more different from Johnson. Stockton was just 6 feet 1. He was not as fast. He was not big. He did not always play with a star-studded lineup during his 19-year NBA career with the Utah Jazz. If Stockton could choose between a pretty but dangerous pass and a simple but smart one, he chose the smart one every time.

Stockton learned to play that way while growing up in Spokane, Washington. He knew he had to outsmart his opponent for his team to win. So Stockton worked on learning where his teammates were supposed to go. That way he knew when to get them the ball with the best chance to score.

Stockton did not play with many stars, but he did have Karl Malone. The big, strong forward was nicknamed "The Mailman" because he always delivered. All Malone needed was the ball and a head of steam. Stockton and Malone were a match made in basketball heaven. They ran the pick-and-roll set to perfection. Stockton would dribble the ball as Malone stepped up to block the player guarding

John Stockton fires a pass as the Lakers' Nick Van Exel, *left*, and Shaquille O'Neal play defense in a 1996 game.

Stockton. The defender had to make a decision. He could chase Stockton or try to guard Malone. Either way Stockton and Malone had the advantage.

The combination worked year after year. Stockton led the NBA in assists a record nine straight seasons. By the middle of his eleventh year in the league, he was closing in on Johnson's mark for career assists.

John Stockton was more than just a great passer. Here he shows his toughness as he drives to the hoop against three Chicago Bulls in the 1997 NBA Finals.

On February 1, 1995, Stockton needed just 11 assists to break Johnson's all-time record. The first 10 came early in the game. In the second quarter, Stockton fed Malone with a bounce pass on the baseline. Malone hit a 17-foot jump shot to give Stockton 9,222 career assists.

Officials stopped the game and Johnson appeared on a video screen. In a taped message he called Stockton "the greatest team leader I have ever played against." Stockton was humble about his record. He said that because he was not the one who made the shots, he should not receive much of the credit.

Stockton was hardly done after that night in 1995. He played through the 2002–03 season. While he never won an NBA championship, he set the career assist record so high it may never be broken. Stockton finished with 15,806 assists. Jason Kidd is second on the list with 12,091.

HANDS OF STEAL

STOCKTON WAS MORE THAN JUST A CRAFTY PASSER. HE HAD SOME OF THE QUICKEST HANDS IN THE NBA. HE USED THOSE HANDS AND HIS BASKETBALL SMARTS TO BECOME A THORN IN THE SIDE OF OPPONENTS ON DEFENSE. STOCKTON LED THE NBA IN STEALS TWICE, AND HIS 3,265 CAREER SWIPES ARE THE MOST EVER. NOT BAD FOR A PLAYER WHO WAS WORRIED HE WAS TOO SLOW AND TOO SMALL TO SUCCEED IN THE NBA.

4

BRILLIANCE
ON THE BENCH

Phil Jackson was a good—but not great—player with the New York Knicks and New Jersey Nets in the 1970s. He moved on to coaching after he retired. He took over as coach of the Chicago Bulls in 1989 and began a journey that ended with 11 NBA titles, the most of any coach in history.

Chicago was led by superstar guard Michael Jordan. The Bulls were talented, but they kept losing in the playoffs. Jackson had to figure out a way for the Bulls to fulfill their potential. Jackson knew he had the right mix of players. The hard part was getting them to play together.

Phil Jackson gives instructions to his Chicago Bulls during the 1991 NBA Finals.

Phil Jackson, *left*, wearing his X hat and one of his championship rings, addresses a crowd of Lakers fans at a 2009 rally as Kobe Bryant, *right*, looks on.

Jackson was different from most coaches. He did not focus too much on drawing up plays. Instead he talked about life and the lessons the game of basketball can teach. Jackson was not very emotional on the bench. Usually he just sat in his chair at the end of the games and smiled proudly after his team won.

Jackson did not always get through to every player, but Jordan was listening. The Bulls won their first NBA title in 1991. They won it again in 1992 and 1993. They briefly left the top when Jordan retired and missed most of the next two years. But Jordan returned, and the Bulls won three straight titles again in 1996, 1997, and 1998.

Jordan retired again after the 1997–98 season, and Jackson took some time off. But one year later the Los Angeles Lakers called. They needed Jackson to do in Los Angeles with center Shaquille O'Neal and guard Kobe Bryant what he had done in Chicago with Jordan.

O'Neal and Bryant were two of the best players in the league in the regular season, but they stumbled in the playoffs. Jackson got his two stars to work better with their teammates. The Lakers won championships in 2000, 2001, and 2002, tying Jackson with Boston's Red Auerbach for the most titles ever by a coach.

In 2009 Jackson finally passed Auerbach when the Lakers beat the Orlando Magic for his tenth title. He wore a hat with the letter X on it in victory. X is the Roman numeral for the number *10*. It was a rare boast for a rare coach. The Lakers won it again the next year, too. Jackson retired in 2011 with 11 NBA titles.

DOUBLE DUTY

AUERBACH AND JACKSON ENJOYED GREAT SUCCESS ON THE BENCH. BUT THEY NEVER DID WHAT BILL RUSSELL DID WITH THE CELTICS IN THE LATE 1960S. RUSSELL TOOK OVER AS BOSTON'S COACH WHEN AUERBACH STEPPED DOWN IN 1966, EVEN THOUGH RUSSELL WAS STILL PLAYING. RUSSELL LED THE CELTICS TO NBA TITLES IN 1968 AND 1969, THE LAST OF THE 11 CHAMPIONSHIPS HE WON DURING HIS PLAYING CAREER. NOBODY HAS WON A TITLE AS A PLAYER/COACH SINCE THEN.

5

A DUNKING SUCCESS

Believe it or not, there was a time when the easiest shot in basketball was against the rules. From 1966–67 to 1976–77 college players were not allowed to take the ball and slam it through the rim for a dunk. If a player's hand touched the rim on a shot attempt, the basket was disallowed.

While dunking was always allowed in the NBA, for years it was something only the tallest players did. That changed in the 1970s and 1980s thanks to a wave of talented, athletic players, led by Julius Erving.

Nate Robinson soars toward the basket during the NBA Slam Dunk Contest in Las Vegas, Nevada, in 2007.

"Dr. J" did more than just dunk. He turned dunking into an art form. Erving could take off far away from the basket, soar through the air, and then jam it home as the crowd rose to its feet.

By the 1980s, everybody was dunking, from 7-foot centers to 6-foot guards. In 1984 the NBA began holding a slam dunk contest the night before the All-Star Game. The dunk contest was the first step to becoming NBA stars for some. Michael Jordan, Dominique Wilkins, and Kobe Bryant each won it early in their careers. In 1988 Jordan and Wilkins held one of the most memorable dunking duels of all time. Jordan won the title by leaping from the foul line all the way to the basket before slamming it home.

As the years passed, finding new ways to impress the judge became tough. Then along came Nate Robinson, who changed the dunk contest forever.

Robinson hardly looked like a guy who could fly through the air. At just 5 feet 9, he was one of the shorter players in the league. But his height did not slow him down. Robinson jumped like he had springs in his legs.

He was a rookie in 2006 when he first stole the show at the dunk contest. Robinson made it to the finals before getting some help for the last round. Former NBA player Spud Webb joined Robinson on the floor. Webb is the smallest dunk contest winner ever, standing just 5 feet 6.

Nate Robinson leaps over former champion Spud Webb to throw one down in the 2006 NBA Slam Dunk Contest in Houston, Texas.

Nate Robinson did not save all his dunks for contests. Here he finishes a reverse slam in a 2009 game against the Atlanta Hawks.

Webb stood in front of the basket and passed the ball to a flying Robinson, who was sailing over Webb's head. Robinson jammed home the alley-oop pass and raised the trophy as the champion. He won it again in 2007, this time without an assist from Webb.

Robinson returned to the dunk contest in 2010 looking to set a record. This time Webb was sitting at the judge's table. Robinson had a tough time early in the contest. He missed several dunks. Finally he saved the day with an awesome slam that he started by throwing the ball off the backboard. He then grabbed it in midair and dunked it with his back to the basket. He was named the winner by a slim vote over the Toronto Raptors' DeMar DeRozan. That gave him the record for most NBA slam dunk titles ever with three.

"I knew I had to try to do dunks that I have not done before," Robinson said. "I had to spice it up a little bit."

Spicing it up was rarely a problem for Robinson, who proved that small guys can fly just as high as big ones.

LONG-DISTANCE LEGEND

THE NBA ADDED A THREE-POINT CONTEST TO ALL-STAR WEEKEND IN 1986. THE BEST SHARPSHOOTERS IN THE LEAGUE COMPETED TO SEE WHO COULD MAKE THE MOST SHOTS IN ONE MINUTE. BOSTON CELTICS FORWARD LARRY BIRD WON THE NBA THREE-POINT SHOOTOUT THE FIRST THREE YEARS IT WAS HELD. THEN CRAIG HODGES TIED THAT RECORD. HODGES WAS A SHARPSHOOTING GUARD WHO PLAYED WITH MICHAEL JORDAN ON THE CHICAGO BULLS IN THE 1980S AND EARLY 1990S. HE WON IT IN 1990, 1991, AND 1992. NO OTHER PLAYER HAS WON IT MORE THAN TWICE. BEFORE THE FIRST CONTEST, BIRD ASKED THE OTHER SHOOTERS WHO WAS COMING IN SECOND BECAUSE HE WAS COMING IN FIRST. "LARRY LEGEND" THEN WENT OUT AND BACKED UP HIS BOAST.

6
HIS AIRNESS
REIGNS

Michael Jordan is one of the greatest basketball players of all time. But even Jordan did not start out on top. Growing up in North Carolina, Jordan was cut by his high school varsity basketball team.

Jordan was a sophomore at Laney High when he tried out for the varsity team. The varsity is made up of the school's best players. Younger players almost always start their careers on the junior varsity. When Jordan failed to make the varsity, he went home and cried. He also made a promise to himself to improve his game.

Jordan did far more than that. He changed basketball. For years the best scorers in the NBA were usually centers. Wilt Chamberlain and Kareem Abdul-Jabbar were big guys who could get close to the hoop. Chamberlain was the NBA's all-time leading scorer when he retired. Abdul-Jabbar passed him in 1984 and is still the league's scoring king.

Jordan was different. He could do a little bit of everything. He could shoot jump shots, and he could dunk. He was not afraid to dribble to the basket and take on the big guys. Jordan always thought he was the best player on the floor. He used each game as a chance to prove it.

After a standout career at the University of North Carolina, Jordan joined the NBA when the Chicago Bulls took him with the third pick in the 1984 draft. He averaged 28.2 points a game as a rookie but missed most of his second season with a foot injury. He used the time off to work on becoming a better all-around player.

By the 1986–87 season, Jordan was unstoppable. No player took more shots. No player made more shots. He led the NBA in scoring that season, averaging 37.1 points a game. That was the first of seven straight scoring titles for Jordan. That tied Chamberlain's record for most seasons leading the NBA in scoring. And while he was piling up the points, the Bulls began piling up victories. Chicago captured the NBA title in 1991, 1992, and 1993 with Jordan leading the way.

Michael Jordan, *right*, drives past Dudley Bradley of the Washington Bullets on October 26, 1984. Jordan was playing in his first NBA game.

Jordan took a break from basketball after the 1992–93 season. He spent a year playing minor league baseball. Jordan was OK with a bat in his hands, but he missed hoops. He returned to the Bulls for the end of the 1994–95 season. Jordan had just turned 32. His legs were getting older, and

Michael Jordan relied on a fierce competitive streak to drive himself to be the best.

he could not fly quite so high. So Jordan changed the way
he played.

He was not quite the player who earned the nickname
"Air Jordan" anymore. He dunked less but made up for

it by playing smarter than his opponents. He used a variety of moves to get open. And when Jordan was open, nobody was better at making baskets. He was a good free-throw shooter, too. If other teams fouled Jordan to try to stop him, he would step to the line and make his free throws.

Jordan averaged 30.4 points in 1995–96 to break Chamberlain's record for most seasons leading the league. Jordan was not done. He was the top scorer each of the next two seasons, too. That pushed the record to 10 years, a full decade. The Bulls won the NBA title in six of those years. And they did it on the back of a player who was still mad about not making the varsity team as a kid.

RAISING THE STAKES

JORDAN AVERAGED 30.1 POINTS PER GAME DURING HIS CAREER. BUT HE WAS EVEN BETTER IN THE PLAYOFFS. JORDAN IS THE NBA'S ALL-TIME LEADING SCORER IN THE POSTSEASON. HE AVERAGED A RECORD 33.4 POINTS IN THE PLAYOFFS. HIS GREATEST GAME EVER CAME AGAINST THE BOSTON CELTICS IN THE 1986 PLAYOFFS. HE POURED IN A RECORD 63 POINTS. THE BULLS LOST IN DOUBLE OVERTIME, BUT JORDAN SENT A MESSAGE. HE WAS ON HIS WAY TO BEING A STAR.

7

A REAL THREE-FOR-ALL

For more than 40 years, taking a shot a long way from the basket in the NBA was a bad idea. All buckets were worth two points. The longer the shot, the less chance you had to make it, right?

That changed in 1979. That year the NBA added the three-point shot as an option for long-distance scoring. A new line was added at each end of the court. The line was 22 feet away from the basket in the corner. At the top of the key, the line was 23 feet 9 inches away from the hoop. Any shot made from behind the line was worth three points.

It took some time for the players to get used to it. Many coaches did not like the three-point line at first, probably because so few players could actually make the shot. In the early days of the three-point line, even good shooters had trouble hitting the shot. Only 28 percent of three-point attempts were good in 1979–80. But the players started to figure it out. Within 10 years, that success rate had risen to 33.1 percent. Another decade later, it was up to 35.3 percent. The three-point experiment was a big hit.

Reggie Miller of the Indiana Pacers was one of the first great three-point shooters. During 18 seasons with the Pacers from 1987–2005, Miller made a record 2,560 three-pointers. But Ray Allen made sure that record did not hold up for long.

Allen was seemingly born to shoot. His form was perfect. Allen would catch the ball and bring it back over his head with his right elbow bent. Then he would let it fly. He did not have a favorite spot on the court. He could connect from just about everywhere. One of Allen's nicknames was "Sugar Ray." That's because his shooting stroke looked so sweet.

Coaches had no problem with letting Allen shoot. He was so good that it seemed like every three-pointer he took would go in. Not all of them did, of course, but Allen kept taking and making more than any player in history.

Ray Allen launches the shot that gave him the NBA record for career three-pointers on February 10, 2011.

Ray Allen, *left*, is congratulated by Reggie Miller after Allen broke Miller's record for career three-pointers on February 10, 2011.

Allen began his NBA career with the Milwaukee Bucks in 1996. He was traded to the Seattle SuperSonics in 2003 and joined the Boston Celtics in 2007. His sharpshooting helped the Celtics win the NBA title in 2008. By the 2010–11 season, he was closing in on Miller's mark for most career three-pointers.

Allen was one behind Miller's total on February 10, 2011, when the Celtics hosted the Los Angeles Lakers, their biggest rival. Allen's first three-pointer hit the rim and rattled out. His second one splashed through the net to tie him with Miller.

Then Allen made the record his. Late in the first quarter, the Celtics were on a fast break. Allen set up a couple of feet behind the three-point line. Teammate Rajon Rondo saw Allen and hit him with a pass. In the blink of an eye, the ball was in the air. Allen watched the ball swish through the hoop from 24 feet away. The home crowd yelled in delight. Allen's mom tried not to cry.

Miller was there, too. During the first break in the action after Allen made his historic basket, Miller stood up and gave Allen a hug.

"All records," Miller said simply, "were made to be broken."

Allen ended the 2013–14 seasons with 2,973 three-pointers, a mark that will be tough to beat.

DOWNTOWN DOMINANCE

RAY ALLEN MIGHT BE THE BEST THREE-POINT SHOOTER EVER. BUT EVEN ALLEN COULD NOT MATCH THE PERFECT NIGHTS THAT LATRELL SPREWELL AND BEN GORDON HAD. SPREWELL AND GORDON SHARE THE NBA RECORD FOR MOST THREE-POINTERS IN A GAME WITHOUT A MISS. THEY EACH WENT 9-FOR-9 FROM BEHIND THE ARC IN A GAME. SPREWELL DID IT IN 2003. GORDON ACTUALLY DID IT TWICE, ONCE IN 2006 AND AGAIN IN 2012.

FUN FACTS

BLOCK PARTY

Hakeem Olajuwon's nickname was "The Dream." But to opponents, Olajuwon, *below*, was a nightmare. The 7-foot center's long arms made it tough for other players to get a shot off. Those who tried often saw Olajuwon swat the ball far, far away. Olajuwon blocked 3,830 shots during his 18-year career, most of them with the Houston Rockets. No other player has more than 3,289.

ROUGH NIGHT

Tim Hardaway was a five-time All-Star during a 15-year career. But one night in 1991, Hardaway had a game to forget. He took 17 shots for the Golden State Warriors that night. He missed every one of them. It's a record for the most shots taken in a game without making one.

KING JAMES

Basketball is a five-man game. It was not for the Cleveland Cavaliers on May 31, 2007. That night it was LeBron James against the Detroit Pistons. James scored 48 points in a 109–107 double-overtime win in Game 5 of the Eastern Conference Finals. "King" James was at his best at the end. He scored Cleveland's final 25 points, a record for the most consecutive points scored by one player.

IRON MAN

Forward A. C. Green was a constant presence on the court during his 15-year career. Green, *above*, played in a record 1,192 consecutive games. The streak stretched from November 19, 1986, until he retired at the end of the 2000–01 season. He played more than 14 straight seasons without taking a day off.

GLOSSARY

alley-oop
A type of shot in which a player leaps in the air, catches a pass from a teammate, and dunks the ball.

assist
A pass that leads directly to a teammate scoring a basket.

blocked shot
A shot deflected from the basket by a defensive player using his hands.

dribble
To move the ball up the floor by bouncing it. A player must dribble it one time for every two steps he takes.

dunk
A basket scored by jamming the ball through the hoop.

playoffs
A competition held after the regular season to determine the league champion.

rebound
To grab a missed shot.

steal
To force a turnover by intercepting or deflecting a pass or dribble of an offensive player.

three-pointer
A shot taken behind the three-point line, which is 23 feet 9 inches from the basket at the top of the key and 22 feet from the basket in the corners.

FOR MORE INFORMATION

Donnelly, Patrick. *The Best NBA Centers of All Time*. Minneapolis, MN: Abdo Publishing, 2014.

Hawkins, Jeff. *Michael Jordan: Basketball Superstar & Commercial Icon*. Minneapolis, MN: Abdo Publishing, 2014.

Silverman, Drew. *The NBA Finals*. Minneapolis, MN: Abdo Publishing, 2013.

WEBSITES

To learn more about Record Breakers, visit **booklinks.abdopublishing.com**. These links are routinely monitored and updated to provide the most current information available.

PLACE TO VISIT

Naismith Memorial Basketball Hall of Fame
1000 Hall of Fame Avenue
Springfield, Massachusetts 01105
(877) 446-6752
www.hoophall.com
A great place to learn about the history of the game, the Naismith Memorial Basketball Hall of Fame is named after Dr. James Naismith, who invented basketball in 1891. The Hall of Fame features interactive exhibits, including skill challenges, live clinics, and shooting contests.

INDEX

ABOUT THE AUTHOR

Will Graves, like Michael Jordan, could not make his varsity basketball team as a sophomore. Unlike Jordan, Graves did not make it as a junior or senior either. Graves settled on writing as a backup plan. He works for the Associated Press in Pittsburgh, Pennsylvania, where he covers the NFL, the NHL, and Major League Baseball when he's not teaching his son how to shoot three-pointers.